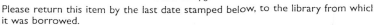

Curriculum Visions

Bromley
THE LONDON BOROUGH
www.bromley.gov.uk

...ans ...ritain

...EDITION

Many interpretations

This book describes some of the things that happened a long time ago. Very little remains of these times and so much of what is said has, of necessity, to be interpretive. In this book the author has tried to present the generally accepted view of historians.

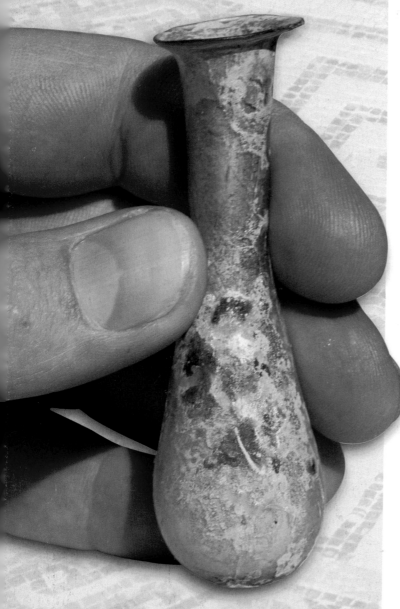

▲ A small perfume bottle, made of Roman glass.

⚠ Look after our heritage!

It is easy to talk about looking after the environment, but we each have to help. Help is often small things, like being careful when you walk around old buildings, and not leaving scratch marks on anything that you visit. It doesn't take a lot of effort – just attitude.

Curriculum Visions

There's more online

See our great collection of page-turning books and multimedia resources at:

www.CurriculumVisions.com

(It's my turn! and The Learning Centre are subscription areas of the web site)

A CVP Book
This second edition © Atlantic Europe Publishing 2010

First edition 2004. First reprint 2005. Second reprint 2006. Third reprint 2007. Fourth reprint 2008. Second edition 2010.

Author
Brian Knapp, BSc, PhD

Editor
Robert Anderson, BA, PGCE

Art Director
Duncan McCrae, BSc

Designed and produced by
Atlantic Europe Publishing

Senior Designer
Adele Humphries, BA, PGCE

Printed in China by
WKT Company Ltd

**The Romans in Britain 2nd edition
– Curriculum Visions
A CIP record for this book is
available from the British Library**

Paperback ISBN 978 1 86214 667 9

Illustrations (c=centre t=top b=bottom l=left r=right)
Kevin Maddison pages 1, 7, 8–9, 20, 24, 33tr, 40, 42; Mark Stacey cover, pages 6, 12, 13, 14, 16, 17, 26, 32b, 35, 36, 38, 41, 43; David Woodroffe pages 11, 15, 22, 23, 25, 29br, 30t, 32t, 39, 44.

Picture credits
All photographs are from the Earthscape Picture Library except the following: (c=centre t=top b=bottom l=left r=right)
© Peter Froste/Museum of London page 30; © Reading Museum Service (Reading Borough Council). All rights reserved. Pages 3cr REDMG:1995.4.1 Euterpe; 3br REDMG:1995.4.1 Silchester Eagle; 3tr REDMG:1962.185.1 Moulsford Torc; 6t REDMG:1995.4.2 Silchester Horse; 34 REDMG:1995.1.103 Silver Spoon; 35tl REDMG:1995.81.31 Samian Ware Bowl; 38cr REDMG:1995.3. Plough share/tip; 39cl REDMG:1995.3. Sheep sheers; 39tr REDMG:1995.3. Roman sickle artefact; 1bl, 45tl REDMG:1995.1.20 Roman writing left behind on a tablet; Painting by Alan Sorrell © English Heritage Photo Library page 28b; Painting by Alan Sorrell © St Albans Museums page 28–29t; © Richard Sorrell/Museum of London page 18–19b.

Acknowledgements
The publishers would like to thank the following for their kind help and advice: English Heritage, The National Trust and Dr Charles Schotman.

This product is manufactured from sustainable managed forests. For every tree cut down at least one more is planted.

Contents

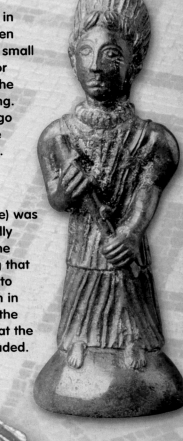

▶ A beautifully crafted Roman torc made from gold. The Celts too were great craftspeople.

▶ This artefact was found in Britain and would have been owned by a Roman. It is a small bronze statue of a muse, or goddess, called Euterpe. She is the patron of flute playing. Euterpe's religious origins go back even further than the Romans to ancient Greece.

▼ This eagle (shown actual size) was cast in bronze. It would originally have had wings. It shows the fine quality of the casting that the Romans were able to make. Britain's wealth in metals was one of the main reasons that the Romans invaded.

Words, names and places

Words in **CAPITALS** are further explained under 'Words, places and names' on pages 46–47.

The Romans in Britain

This book is about the Romans – a people who lived about 2,000 years ago. The Romans built a vast empire, which for more than 400 years included Britain.

Here is a summary of what happened in Britain during Roman times.

1 About 2,000 years ago the **ROMANS** came to Britain from Italy, a land on the edge of the Mediterranean far to the east of the British Isles. Rome was the capital of the Roman **EMPIRE**.

2 The Romans were one of world's most powerful people. Their strong leaders and well-trained army **CONQUERED** much of Europe and created a great empire.

3 The Romans first sent an army to Britain in 55 BC under **JULIUS CAESAR**, but this army stayed only briefly.

4 A much larger Roman army returned in AD 43 under **CLAUDIUS** and conquered all of Britain. The army was too small to keep control of all the country and it eventually retreated from most of Scotland and built **HADRIAN'S WALL**.

5 The Romans built roads, forts, fine houses and many great public buildings such as temples and **AMPHITHEATRES**.

> **BC and AD**
> BC is shorthand for 'before Christ' and indicates that a date is before the traditional date of the birth of Jesus Christ. For example: 55 BC.
> AD is shorthand for the latin *Anno Domini*, which means 'in the year of our Lord'. It shows that a date is after the traditional date of the birth of Jesus Christ. For example: AD 55.

▼ All civilisations have a way to pay for goods. The Romans used coins as shown below. The Celts had coins, too.

As
The Roman unit of currency was the as. This one-as coin shows the Roman emperor Gaius Caesar – better known by his nickname, Caligula. This coin dates from between AD 37 and 41.

Dupondius
Worth two asses. This example shows the emperor Trajan, who ruled between AD 98 and 117. This coin dates from between AD 103 and 111.

Sestertius
Worth four asses. This bronze example shows a portrait of the Roman emperor Hadrian, who reigned between AD 117 and 138. The coin dates from AD 126 to 138.

6 The Romans made Britain a province (region) of the empire that could supply them with useful goods, such as tin.

7 Most of Britain's native peoples – we will call them the **BRITISH** – lived in the countryside. The Romans built towns and country houses (**VILLAS**) to live in. The Romans mainly mixed only with the British chiefs.

8 The Romans never allowed the British to rule themselves. They also sometimes treated the British harshly, and this led to revolts. The most famous revolt was led by Queen **BOUDICCA** in AD 60.

9 As Roman power weakened at the beginning of the fifth century AD, the Romans began to take their army away. The British were left unprepared to protect themselves against more **INVADERS**.

Front Back

Denarius
Worth 16 asses. This example is from the time of Julius Caesar and dates from 49 to 48 BC. The front of the coin represents good (the elephant) trampling evil on the back (the serpent).

Aureus
Worth 100 asses. From the period of emperor Claudius from AD 41 to 54.

ROMANS IN BRITAIN TIMELINE

250 BC	Invasion of Britain by Celtic people (CELTS) from France.
222 BC	The Romans begin to conquer more land, starting with northern Italy.
218 BC	Hannibal crosses the Alps with elephants.
170 BC	Rome has paved streets for the first time.
146 BC	The Roman empire now includes North Africa, Greece, Spain and France. Some Celts from France (the Belgics) flee to Britain.
55 BC	Emperor Julius Caesar enters Britain.
AD 5	The Romans treat Cymbeline, the king of a powerful British tribe, the Catuvellauni, as king of England, even though he only controls the south.
AD 43	LEGIONS under emperor Claudius invade Britain, and defeat the British army under CARACTACUS at the Battle of Medway. The Romans found London. The new land (an imperial province) is named BRITANNIA.
AD 51	Caractacus captured.
AD 60	Queen Boudicca of the Iceni tribe revolts and sacks London.
AD 78	Roads and forts built in Wales.
AD 82	Roman governor AGRICOLA completes the conquest of Britain and reaches northern Scotland (CALEDONIA).
AD 87	Scottish Highlands abandoned.
AD 105	Scottish Lowlands abandoned.
AD 122	Emperor HADRIAN pulls troops from Scotland and has Hadrian's Wall built across northern England.
AD 140	Emperor ANTONINUS PIUS advances back to the rivers Forth and Clyde in Scotland and has the ANTONINE WALL built.
AD 163	Antonine Wall abandoned.
AD 180	The Romans are defeated by Scottish 'BARBARIANS' (PICTI) and Hadrian's Wall overrun.
AD 205	Hadrian's Wall rebuilt.
AD 217	Britain peaceful and prosperous to 275 when Saxon raids begin.
AD 287	Carausius, who commands the Roman fleet defending Britain, rebels against Rome and declares himself emperor of Britain.
AD 306	Emperor Constantine supervises the rebuilding of Britain. Peace and prosperity until AD 342.
AD 342	Barbarian attacks become more frequent.
AD 350	Walls are built around many cities.
AD 360	Major attacks by Picti and SCOTTI on northern England. These are driven back in AD 370 by emperor Theodosius.
AD 383	Roman legions begin to leave Britain in order to protect Italy from invasion.
AD 410	The Roman emperor Honorius declared to the people of Britannia that they had to "look after their own defence".
AD 425	British have to pay for the help of Saxons, Jutes and Angles from Germany to expel Picti and Scotti (Irish).
AD 457	The British are gradually defeated by the Angles, Saxons and Jutes and many retreat west to Wales. Britain is divided into small kingdoms again.

The British

The British were the people who lived in Britain before the Romans. They were a country people, living close to hilltop forts.

▲ ② **This brooch is an example of the metalware made by the Celts. It was one way of wearing your wealth.**

The **BRITISH** people who had lived in Britain had been there for hundreds of years before the Romans arrived about 2,000 years ago.

What the British were like

The British, who some people call **CELTS**, were farming people who grew corn and kept pigs, goats, sheep and cattle. Although there were many different **TRIBES** (kingdoms), the people all spoke the same language and shared a common history.

Men or women could become rulers of their tribe. Below the rulers came a small group of nobles. They were warriors whose job was to fight to protect the tribe (picture ①). Some nobles became the tribe's priests and teachers, and were known as **DRUIDS**.

Everybody else worked on the farms, or made pottery, clothing and metal goods. The British did not have slaves. However, in general, not even the nobles could read or write.

◀ ① **The relatively simple armour worn by the Celts. Much of it was leather.**

Skilled craftspeople

Consequently the British have left little in writing to tell us about their lives. However, we do know that British peoples were skilled in many crafts because, at important funerals the possessions of the dead person were buried with them. Items made of wood and cloth have rotted away, but items made out of metal have survived. This is enough for us to see that the British were very skilled and could make beautiful objects, such as jewellery and swords (pictures ① and ②).

▼ ③ **British, or Celtic, farmhouses were small, round houses with a thatched roof and a fire in the centre. There was just one room, home to a whole family.**

British people built great earthen forts on hilltops. They are called Iron Age forts and are often marked on maps as 'camps'. Here people could live during troubled times. The forts were, however, no protection against the Roman army, as you will see on page 10.

Homes and forts

People normally lived in clusters of small round houses close to their fields and animals (picture ③).

Living in these times was dangerous because kingdoms were often at war with one another.

To protect themselves tribes built large oval-shaped **FORTS** on hilltops. Soil was dug out of the ground to make ditches near the hilltop. The soil was put next to each ditch to make an earth wall. The biggest forts had several ditches and walls. Here the people also kept stores of food.

Although the British fought among themselves, for about 600 years nobody attacked them from overseas. However, this was to change in 55 BC when the Romans arrived!

A hole in the roof let the smoke out

Wooden fences for protection

The Romans

**The Romans spread their way of life across their empire.
Britain lay on the edge of this empire.**

The Romans were a **WARRIOR** people who were always ruled by men. They got much of their wealth by **CONQUERING** other peoples.

▼ ① **Ancient Rome was the centre of a very powerful empire and its buildings showed the wealth it had collected from the people and lands it ruled. Roman buildings were similar to those designed by the ancient Greeks. Rome was built on a grand scale. Columns, arches, vaults and domes made the city look impressive.**

How Romans gained new land

The Romans kept a large army of paid soldiers (see pages 12 and 13). This was very different from other peoples, who only formed an army when they were attacked. The Roman armies were made of groups of soldiers called **LEGIONS**. The commander of all the legions was the **EMPEROR**.

Because the Roman **EMPIRE** was so large, parts of the empire were ruled by **GOVERNORS**. A governor was put in charge of Britain.

How Romans lived in Rome

Wealthier Romans lived in towns. Here they could go to visit entertainments in a great oval building with tiers of seats called an **AMPHITHEATRE** (pages 36 and 37), or meet and talk in the market-place called a **FORUM** (pictures ① and ②).

◀▼ ② **Although ancient Rome has been destroyed and rebuilt many times you can still see many remains today.**

Because the army was so important, emperors made sure that the soldiers were well paid. Soldiers were among the wealthiest people in the empire.

The wealthy owned large areas of land in the countryside, called **ESTATES,** and lived in large country houses called **VILLAS** (pages 40 and 41).

The estates were the places where the food was produced. It took many people to grow food, so most lived and worked in the countryside.

The Romans also used **SLAVES**. Slaves were people taken from lands that the Romans had conquered.

Romans bring their way of life to Britain

When the Romans came to Britain, they brought the Roman way of life with them. Wealthy Romans, including retired commanders of the army, lived in luxury in the British countryside. There they built farmhouses which were like the Roman villas in Italy. Others lived in the new towns the Romans built.

Most Romans never intended to settle down in Britain. Although many soldiers married British wives the Romans mostly lived apart from the native British.

The Roman invasions

The Romans wanted the wealth of Britain. However, they did not find the country easy to conquer.

Rome had traded with the British for many years and even the Roman language, **LATIN**, was used by a few British kingdoms on their coins. But on the 26th of August 55 BC the Roman emperor **JULIUS CAESAR**, decided to make Britain part of the Roman empire.

Ten thousand Romans landed near Dover. Some of the British welcomed the Romans and were friendly to them, but others – especially the more powerful tribes – did not want the Romans in Britain and so they fought back.

The British believed their hilltop forts would serve them well against any attack, but they had not bargained for the power of the Roman army. The Romans burned the gates down or surrounded the hill forts, forcing the British to starve or surrender.

The British were soon overpowered and forced to make peace and send a kind of yearly **TAX** called a **TRIBUTE** to Rome.

However, only a year after they arrived, the Roman army left again to fight elsewhere in their vast empire.

The return of the Romans

Britain was a country rich in wool, tin and other metals. It could be made to produce a lot of grain. In AD 43 the Roman emperor,

▲ ① **Claudius ruled the Roman empire from AD 41 to 54.**

CLAUDIUS (picture ①), brought a powerful army and called the new colony **BRITANNIA** (picture ②).

Why the British were beaten

When Claudius' army arrived, some of the tribes were friendly, but others were not. Those who decided to fight had little experience at forming large armies and the men were brave, but poorly trained. One of these tribes was led by Caractacus and you can find out about him on pages 14 and 15.

The British only fought when they were not needed on the farms. This made it much easier for the well-trained full-time Roman soldiers to beat them.

The Romans won Britain partly by fighting, but also by showing friendly British leaders that life would be better under Roman rule.

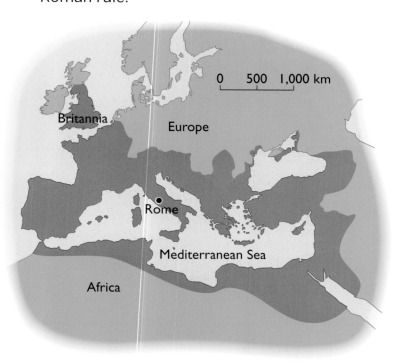

▲ ② Britain, which the Romans called Britannia, was on the edge of the Roman empire. It was not particularly important to the Romans and often hard to defend.

Invasion brings change

As soon as the Romans conquered a region they began building forts, then roads, then towns as each emperor made his mark on the British scene (pictures ③ and ④). These are new to the British way of life.

The purpose of the Roman invasion was to take some of the wealth from Britain back to Rome. But the invasion also brought good things: a better standard of living for many of those nobles who chose to work with the Romans, better education and a more stable country.

▼ ④ Emperor TRAJAN is commemorated with a statue by the Roman wall in London (see page 31).

◀ ③ Emperor HADRIAN, one of the few bearded emperors (see pages 24 and 25).

The Roman army

The Roman army was made of full-time soldiers who were very well trained.

The Roman army was made of multi-skilled soldiers. When they were not fighting, the soldiers built walls and forts, laid out towns, built roads and even became temporary teachers and tax collectors.

Centurions and legions

The Roman army was divided into **LEGIONS** each containing 6,000 men called **LEGIONARIES** (picture ①). Each legion was divided into smaller units of 100 men, each commanded by a **CENTURION** (picture ②).

The Romans also used **AUXILIARIES**. These were soldiers brought from places outside Rome. They were usually led by Romans.

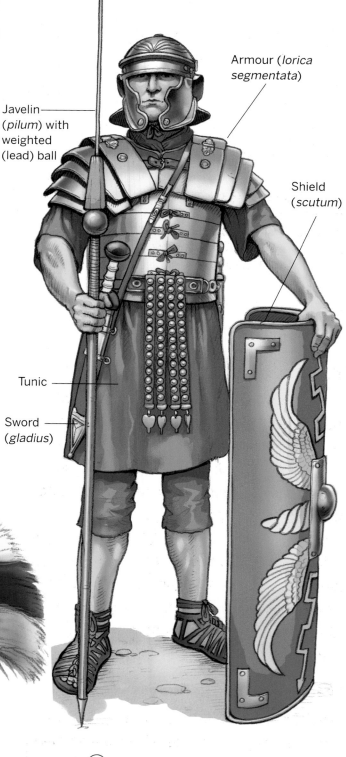

Javelin (*pilum*) with weighted (lead) ball

Armour (*lorica segmentata*)

Shield (*scutum*)

Tunic

Sword (*gladius*)

▶ ② A centurion's helmet. The helmet was made of iron. It had a fan of horsehair across the top and cheek plates down the sides. A metal strap hooked below the chin.

▲ ① The dress of a Roman soldier. The Roman soldier had armour made of metal plates that protected the upper part of the body. Notice the gladius (sword) on the waist belt and the javelin in the hand. The ordinary soldier did not have a fan of horsehair like the centurion.

▲ ③ Romans used many military techniques. In this 'tortoise' (testudo) formation they protected themselves from arrows using their shields.

▼ ④ The Romans learned how to attack from a distance using javelins before they used their swords.

Army dress

The Roman soldier wore a woollen tunic that had short sleeves and came down to just above the knees.

To protect himself in battle he also wore a metal helmet and had metal plates protecting his upper body. He carried a wooden shield (picture ③), and he fought with a short sword called a *gladius*, a dagger and one or more throwing spears called javelins (picture ①). The javelins were thrown at the attackers before they got within sword reach (picture ④).

Army pay

The legionary was a full-time soldier and was paid regular wages. He was also paid a share of any spoils from the conquering of new lands.

When he retired, the soldier was given a pension. As a result, being a soldier was a very attractive job in Roman times.

Roman forts

The Romans ruled Britain from **FORTS**. Forts were large and many could house an entire legion (pages 20 and 21).

Inside the fort were stores of food, weapons, a hospital and living quarters for the troops.

The troops sometimes brought their families and these lived in houses just outside the fort walls. There was also an **AMPHITHEATRE** for entertainment and temples for worship.

How big was the army?

For many years the Romans kept an army of 55,000 men in Britain. In the early days they were needed to conquer the country, then they were needed to keep out tribes from Scotland, Ireland and Europe. They called all of the people outside the empire **BARBARIANS**.

Caractacus fights to stay free

Caractacus was a brave tribal leader who resisted the Roman invasion. In the end he was captured by another British tribe.

There were some famous and very brave Britons who did not want to live under the Romans. One of these was called **CARACTACUS**.

Caractacus led an army made up of people from a number of tribes who tried to stop the Roman invasion (picture ①).

▼ ① Caractacus and his army fight the Romans in AD 43. They soon discover just how well trained and armed the Roman army is and Caractacus is forced to retreat.

The army of Caractacus was made of part-time soldiers who had not trained together. They were no match for the Romans and so they were forced to retreat further and further west. Eventually, the small army with Caractacus had to live in the Welsh hills and could only make hit and run (guerilla) attacks on the Romans.

Caractacus kept up these hit and run raids for nine years.

Early Britain

The Romans did not, at first, mean to capture all of Britain, and to begin with, they advanced only to a line between Exeter and the River Humber. They built a road along this line so that it was easy for their troops to get to places of trouble. They called this road Fosse Way (picture (2)) (see page 23).

Advances into Wales

However, Caractacus, along with other tribes in Wales, was still causing trouble along the border, so the Romans decided the only way to deal with the trouble was to conquer all of England and Wales (picture (2)). This they did by AD 79.

Betrayed

The Romans still could not capture Caractacus, so they had to make a deal with another of the British tribes called the Brigantes.

If the Brigantes could hand Caractacus over, then the Romans would look favourably

on them. So when Caractacus was next in the lands of the Brigantes – who he thought were friendly to him – they captured him and handed him to the Romans.

Courage recognised

The Romans took Caractacus and his family to Rome. Here he expected to be executed. However, emperor Claudius admired his courage and so pardoned him. Nevertheless, they never let him return to Britain in case he might cause trouble again.

▼ (2) **The stages of the Roman invasion of Britain. (The Romans did not invade Ireland.)**

Caledonia

0   50   100 km

AD 80
AD 79
AD 49–78
AD 43–47

Hibernia

BRIGANTES

York

ORDOVICES   CORIELTAVI   ICENI

CATUVELLAUNI

TRINOVANTES

SILURES

Fosse Way

DOBUNI

ATREBATES

DUROTRIGES   BELGAE

Exeter

DUMNONII

Differing ways of life

The Romans lived very different ways of life and had different beliefs from the British. As a result, there was often an uneasy peace between them.

Britain became an imperial province of Rome and the British were ruled by the Romans.

The Romans and the British were such different people, there were many chances for misunderstandings. Here are some of their differences.

We cannot understand the language the Romans speak. Only a few of us have been taught Latin.

The Celtic view

We have always been ruled by kings and queens. We are loyal to our rulers and we like them to sort out our problems. We have no need for foreign laws and courthouses. We are used to dealing with each problem as it comes up.

The Romans think we are second-class citizens.

We do not have slaves. All of our people are free.

We live in the countryside and have little use for towns.

Our priests are called Druids. If the spirits are angry they will offer a human sacrifice.

We believe our gods are spirits that are everywhere around us. We have spirits in trees, lakes, rivers and mountains.

We have a strict set of rules telling us how to live our lives. It is called the rule of law.

We believe in gods that are like people. Jupiter is the most important god. He is the god of the heavens and responsible for thunder and lightning and other terrible natural events.

Mars is the second most important god. He is the bringer of war. Other important gods are Juno and Minerva, but there are many others.

The Roman view

We think human sacrifice is a terrible thing.

We believe in the rule of law. The British have never had any laws, so we must make them obey ours.

We often make captured people into slaves. How else would we get people to do all of the hard work?

The British are second-class citizens because they have been conquered.

We think that a good way to keep the British peaceful is to make their rulers more wealthy and more like Roman citizens.

Boudicca rebels

Some Britons were treated badly by the Romans and so they rebelled. The most famous was a queen – Boudicca.

The Romans mainly tried to work with the rulers of the tribes they had captured. In this way there was less likely to be trouble from them. However, they insisted that the natives carried no weapons. This was, of course, quite against the traditions of the native tribes.

The Romans also expected to get the lands and money of the British rulers as soon as they died. But this was not, of course, what the family of the rulers expected.

Worst of all, the Romans were not used to dealing with women leaders, as women were not allowed to hold important positions in Rome. In Britain they decided to put up with this difficulty – for a while.

Boudicca rebels

Trouble flared just 17 years after the invasion when the king of the Iceni, a British tribe in the east, died. His wife – **BOUDICCA** (also spelled Boadicea) became queen (pictures ① and ②).

The Romans used the king's death as an excuse to take over the tribe's lands and stop Boudicca becoming queen.

▼ ① Boudicca was a queen of the Iceni tribe. Her fight to stand up for her rights has been seen as a symbol for British people through the ages. They sacked London killing thousands of people and burned buildings as they went.